iPhone 11

The iPhone Manual for Beginners, Seniors & for All
iPhone Users (Tips & Tricks Version)
(The Simplified Manual for Kids and Adults)
3rd Edition

Dale Brave

ISBN: 978-1-63750-242-6

Table of Contents

Introduction

The iPhone 11, iPhone 11 Pro, and iPhone 11 Pro Max are faster than ever and have more powerful cameras. With the latest edition of this bestselling guide, you get a funny, simplified guide to the tips, shortcuts, and workarounds that will turn you into an iPhone master.

For those who want the most sophisticated technology available in a mobile phone, but without a sky-high price, the iPhone 11 made from surgical-grade stainless steel with a selection of colors to choose from, and a double-lens camera array at the back is the best mobile phone available to date.

Millions of people all over the world are excited about this new iPhone 11, iPhone 11 pro and iPhone 11 Pro Max, simply because the iPhone offers many advance and exciting features, including a *camera like no other*, *Siri*, turn-by-turn driving directions, a calendar, and a lot more. But if you're acquiring the iPhone 11 and iPhone 11 Pro and iPhone 11 Pro Max, for the first time, or you probably need more information on how to use your device optimally, that is why this book is your best choice of guide.

In this book you'll discover:

- How to set up your brand new iPhone
- iPhone 11 Series Security Features
- Apple Face ID Hidden Features
- All iPhone 11 Gestures you should know
- How to Hide SMS notification content display on iPhone screen
- Software & hardware features of iPhone 11
- In-depth coverage of iOS 13
- Top iPhone gestures and shortcuts
- Difference between iPhone 11 & iPhone X
- Detailed camera app tutorials
- The secrets of mastering mobile photography
- Troubleshooting tips
- How to use the virtual Home button
- How to enable limited USB settings
- Best Shortcuts you are never aware of
- Disabling Location-Based iAds
- How to Use Look Around feature in Apple Maps

- How to Customize Your Memoji and Animoji
- How to Use the New Gestures for Copy, Cut, Paste, Redo and Undo
- How to Use Cycle Tracking in Health

...and a lot more.

It is the perfect guide for all iPhone users, as you would get simplified follow-through in-depth tips and tutorials on every possible thing you should know about iPhone 11, iPhone 11 pro and iPhone 11 Pro Max.

Chapter 1

How to Set up Your brand-new iPhone 11

For many individuals, the iPhone 11 Series would radically not be the same as the previous iPhone model. Not surprisingly, the iPhone set up process hasn't transformed much. However, you might end up on the familiar ground; you may still find a lot of little things you honestly must do before you switch ON your new phone for the very first time (or soon after that).

Let's check out how to set up your brand-new iPhone 11 the proper way.

Setup iPhone 11 the Correct Way

With iPhone 11, you'll have the ability to take benefit of Apple's Automatic Setup. If you're on an updated iPhone without Face Identification, you would see that Touch ID is entirely gone. (Which means you'll save one face, rather than several.)

If you're a serial upgrader, and you're from the year-old iPhone X, less has changed. But you'll still need to update just as usual.

iPhone 11 Set up: The Fundamentals

Re-download only the applications you would need; that one is crucial. Most of us have so many applications on our iPhones that people do not use; this is the big reason we execute a clean set up, in all honesty. Utilize the App Store application and make sure you're authorised into the Apple accounts. (Touch the tiny icon of the Updates - panel to see which accounts you're logged on to.) Only download applications you've found in the past half a year. Or, be daring: download stuff you Utilize regularly. We're prepared to wager it'll be considered a very few.

Set up *DO NOT Disturb* - If you're like ordinary people, you're constantly getting notifications, iMessages, and other types of distractions through to your iPhone.

Create *DO NOT Disturb* in the Configurations application (it's in the next section listed below, slightly below *Notifications* and *Control Centre*). You'll want to routine it for occasions when you need never to be bothered.

Toggle Alarm to On and then Messages when you want to keep Notifications away from that person. Try 9 p.m. to 8 a.m. when you can.

Pro suggestion: *Let some things through if there's an Emergency: Enable Allow Phone calls From your Favourites and toggle Repeated Phone calls to On. iOS 13 also enables you to switch on DO NOT Disturb at Bedtime, which mutes all notifications and even hides them from the lock screen, and that means you don't get distracted when you take the phone to check the time.*

Auto Setup for iPhone 11

Secondly; Auto Setup enables you to duplicate your Apple ID and home Wi-Fi configurations from another device, simply by getting them close collectively.

In case your old iPhone (or iPad) has already been operating iOS 12 or iOS 13, to put it simply the devices next to one another. Then follow the prompts to avoid needing to enter your Apple ID and Wi-Fi passwords; this makes the original iPhone set up much smoother.

Set up a fresh iPhone 11 from Scratch

The guide below assumes you're establishing your brand-new iPhone from scratch. If you don't wish to accomplish that, you'll need to acquire any of the other iPhone manuals for beginners that I have written.

Restoring from a back-up of Your old iPhone

You'll probably be restoring your brand-new iPhone from a back-up of your present iPhone. If that's so, then you merely want to do a couple of things:

- Be sure you come with an up-to-date backup.

- Use Apple's new Auto Setup feature to get you started.

The first thing is as simple as going to the iCloud configurations on your iPhone, and looking at that, they're surely a recent automated back-up. If not, do one by hand. Head to *Configurations* > *Your Name* > *iCloud* > *iCloud Back-up and tap* **BACKUP Now**. Wait around until it is done.

Set up Face ID

Face ID is much simpler to use than Touch ID, and it's also simpler to create. Instead of needing to touch your iPhone with your fingerprints, one at a time, you simply check out the camera, and that's almost it. To create Face ID on your iPhone, do the next when prompted through the preliminary iPhone setup. (If you'd like to begin over with a phone you set up previously, check out *Settings > Face ID & Passcode, and type in your password, to begin.*)

Establishing Face ID is similar to the compass calibration your iPhone enables you to do from time to time when you use the Maps app. Only rather than rolling the iPhone around, you turn your head. You'll need to do two scans, and then the iPhone 11 would have your 3D head stored in its Secure Enclave, inaccessible to anything, even to iOS itself (despite some clickbait "news" stories).

Now, still, in Settings/*Configurations > Face ID & Passcode*, you can pick which features to use with Face ID, as everyone else did with *Touch ID*.

If you regularly sport another appearance - you're a clown, a doctor, an impersonator, or something similar -

then additionally, you should create another impression. Just tap the button in the facial ID settings to set this up.

Create iPhone Email

- *Add your email accounts* - Whether you utilize Mail, Perspective, or something similar to Sparrow, you'll want to include your email accounts immediately. For Apple's Email app, touch *Configurations > Accounts & Passwords, then tap Add Accounts.* Choose your email supplier and follow the steps to enter all the knowledge required.

- *See more email preview* - Email lets you start to see the content of a note without starting it. May as well see as a lot of it as you possibly can, right? Utilize Settings > Email and tap on the Preview button. Change your configurations to five lines and get more information from your email messages and never have to get them open up.

- *Established your default accounts* - For reasons unknown, our iOS Email settings always appear to default to a merchant account we never use, like *iCloud*. Tap *Configurations > Accounts & Passwords > Your email accounts name, and then touch Accounts > Email.* Once you reach the depths of the settings, you can touch your preferred email; this would be your address in new mails. (When there is only one address in here, you're all set.) That is also the spot to add some other email addresses associated with your email account.

Advanced iPhone Email tweaks

- *Swipe to control email* - It's much more helpful to have the ability to swipe your email messages away rather than clicking through and tapping on several control keys. Swipe to Archive, so that whenever you swipe that path, you'll have the ability to either quickly save a contact to your Archive. Or, if your email accounts support swiping left as a default Delete action, it'll offer a Garbage icon. Swipe left to Tag as Read, which is a smart way to slam through your electronic mails as you have them. This only impacts your built-in

Email application from Apple. Each third-party email customer can do things differently.

- *Add an HTML signature* - A sound email signature really can cause you to look professional, so make sure to include an HTML signature to your email. If you've already got one on the desktop, duplicate and paste the code into contact and ahead to yourself.

You'll be able to copy and paste it into an Email application (or whichever email supplier you like, if it facilitates it). It could be as easy as textual content formatting tags or as complicated as adding a logo design from a webserver. You should use an iOS application to make one, too; however, they tend to look fairly basic.

Manage Calendars, iCloud, Communications and more

- *Set default Calendar alert times* - Calendar is ideal for alerting you to important occasions, but it's not necessarily at a convenient or useful time.

Established the default timing on three types of occasions: Birthdays, Occasions, and All-Day Occasions, and that means you get reminders when they're helpful. Utilize *Configurations* > *Calendars*. Tap on Default Alert Times and set your Birthday reminders to 1 day before, your Occasions to quarter-hour before (or a period which makes more sense to your mind), and All-Day Occasions on the day of the function (10 a.m.). You'll never miss a meeting again.

- ***Background application refresh*** - You'll desire to be selective about which applications you desire to be in a position to run in the background, so have a look at the list in *Settings* > *General* > *Background App Refresh*. Toggle Background App Refresh to ON, then toggle OFF all the applications you don't need being able to access anything in the background. When in question, toggle it to OFF and find out if you are slowed up by any applications that require to refresh when you release them. You'll want to allow

Background Refresh for Cult of Macintosh Magazine!

Secure Your Web Experience

- *Browser set up* - Surfing the net is filled with forms to complete. Adding your name, address, email, and bank cards may take up a great deal of your power. Make sure to head into Configurations > Browser > AutoFill to create your mobile internet browser the proper way. First, toggle Use Contact Info to On. Then tap on My Info and select the contact you want to use when you encounter form areas in Browser. Toggle Titles and Passwords on as well, and that means you can save that across appointments to the same website. (This pulls from *iCloud Keychain*, so make sure to have that allowed, too.)

Toggle *CREDIT CARDS* to ON as well, which means you can shop swiftly. (*be sure only to use SSL-encrypted websites.*)

Pro suggestion: Manage which bank cards your iPhone

helps you to save with a tap on BANK CARDS. You can include new cards within, or delete ones that no more work or that you don't want to use via mobile Browser.

The browser in iOS 13 and later version also blocks cross-site monitoring, which are those cookies that follow you around and let online stores place the same advertisements on every subsequent web page you visit. That is On by default, and that means you should not do anything. Just relax and revel in your newfound personal privacy.

iCloud Everywhere

- *iCloud is everything* - There's without a doubt in our thoughts that iCloud is the easiest, optimum solution for keeping all of your stuff supported and safe. Utilize the Configurations > iCloud and be sure to register with your **Apple ID**. You can manage your storage space in here, but make sure to enable all you need immediately. Enable iCloud Drive, Photos, Connections, Reminders, Browser, Records, News, Wallet, Back-up, Keychain and others once you get the iPhone unpacked. You can enable Email and Calendars if you merely use Apple's applications and services; usually, you would keep those toggled OFF.

Services subscription during iPhone setup

- *Enable iCloud Photo Library* - We love the iCloud Photo Library. It maintains your photos and videos securely stored in the cloud and enable you to get full-quality copies of your documents in the event you misplace your originals. iCloud Picture Library depends on your iCloud storage space, if you have a lot of photos, you'll want to bump that up. Utilize Configurations > iCloud > Photos, then toggle iCloud Image Library to On. (Remember that this will switch off My Picture Stream. If you'd like both, you'll need to re-toggle Image Stream back again to On.)

- *Use iTunes Match* - Sure, Apple Music monitors all the music data files on your devices, but if you delete them from your iPhone and don't have a back-up elsewhere, you're heading to have to stay for whatever quality Apple Music will provide you with when you listen. If you wish to maintain your full-resolution music documents supported to the cloud, use iTunes Match.

You get all of your music files matched up or published to iCloud in the best bitrate possible. After that, you can stream or download the music to any device provided your iTunes Match membership is intact. Never be without your music (or have an over-filled iPhone) again. Go to *Configurations > Music.* Then touch on Sign up to iTunes Match to understand this valuable service allowed on your brand-new iPhone.

More iPhone set up Tweaks

- ***Extend your Auto-Lock*** - Let's face it. The default two minutes you get for the Volume of time your iPhone would remain on without turning off its screen may keep the battery higher much longer, but it's insufficient for anybody during regular use.

Utilize Configurations, General, Auto-Lock to create this to the whole five minutes, which means you can stop tapping your screen at all times to keep it awake.

- *Get texts everywhere* - You can enable your Mac PC or iPad to get texts from your iPhone, provided you've set up iMessage to them (Settings, Text messages, toggle iMessage to ON on any iOS device, Messages Preferences on your Mac). Ensure that your other device is close by when you Utilize Settings on your iPhone, then touch Messages > TEXT Forwarding. Any devices available will arrive on the list. Toggle your Mac or iPad to On, and then check the prospective device for a code. Enter that code into your iPhone. Now all of your devices are certain to get not only iMessages but also texts from those not using iMessage.

- *Equalise your tunes* - Start the EQ in your Music application to be able to hear your preferred jams and never have trouble with a Bluetooth speaker.

Go to Configurations > Music. Once there, touch on EQ and established your iPhone to NIGHT TIME; this will provide you with a great quantity rise for those times where you want to blast *The Clash* while you make a quick supper in the kitchen.

Chapter 2
iPhone 11 Pro Overview

Home devices are so organic. It's a disservice to see them through an individual attribute; for instance, calling the iPhone 11 Pro and iPhone 11 Pro Max "cell phones" or even smartphones is reductive. At best, they're pocketable computer systems with communication, content catch, and posting with efficient features.

Yet, when people navigate the new handsets, which Apple unveiled on Sept 10 in Cupertino, CA, all they can easily see is the three-camera zoom lens construction seated in an elevated cup square on the trunk of every device.

iPhone 11 Pro and iPhone 11 Pro Max

Apart from size, the iPhone 11 Pro (foreground) and the iPhone 11 Pro Max are identical electronically. They are Reduced to a meme, the iPhone 11 Pro and iPhone Pro Max might run into a significant misstep in Apple's decade-plus through smartphone developing design and development jobs, but that might be a misreading of reality.

Studying a large number of friendly media responses to my first photos of the 5.8-inch iPhone 11 Pro and 6.5-inch iPhone 11 Pro Max, I became confident of the fact that the merchandise looked different in pictures than it looks physically. Why I wouldn't call the camera square beautiful; it is durable, telegraphing its photographic motives and features to anyone who cares.

Apart from the radical camera component redesign, Apple didn't stray the iPhone body design, vocabulary introduced with the iPhone 6, which has continued to last years before iPhone XS. Apple's iPhone 11 Pro ($999, 64 GB) and 11 Pro Max ($1,099 64 GB) feature lots of the same recognizable curves on the iPhone XS.

Bottom level end of the iPhone 11 Pro and iPhone 11 Pro Max

Apple hasn't transformed the port, mic, or speaker settings on the iPhone 11 Pro and iPhone 11 Pro Max. Departing aside for an instant, the display technology changes; Apple didn't even change the display screen design, all of the new iPhones still feature the TrueDepth notch within a normally unblemished, almost edge-to-edge display.

iPhone 11 Pro in Hand

Aside from an original 12 MP camera, the real Depth notch is unchanged.   However, what will be more noticeable within the last couple of years is that these new devices have added on just a little weight. Apple does not focus on the weight and width of their iPhones, in virtually any meaningful way. That's because being the thinnest didn't gain them anything (keep in mind when individuals were purposely twisting their 6.9 mm-thin iPhones?).

At 144 mm high by 71.4 mm wide by 8.1 mm deep, the

5.8-inch iPhone 11 Pro is slightly bigger than the iPhone XS and noticeably thicker than last year's 7.7 mm smartphone. The story plot is the same on the bigger 6.5-inch iPhone 11 Pro Max. It's 158 mm by 77.8 mm by 8.1 mm thick. With 226 grams, it's 18 grams heavier than the iPhone XS Max.

iPhone 11 Pro Stacked atop iPhone 11 Pro Max

The iPhone 11 Pro and iPhone 11 Pro Max are somewhat thicker, larger, and more substantial than the XS series. Dimension-wise, the new iPhone 11 Pro and iPhone 11 Pro max don't feel much different; however, the added width and weight are unmistakable and don't even try to evaluate it to a bigger-screen 6.8-inch Samsung Galaxy Notice10+. Samsung's handset is both slimmer (7.9 mm) and significantly lighter (196 grams) than small-screened iPhone 11 Pro Max, while still including an S-Pen stylus.

iPhone 11 Pro held aloft in hand

The iPhone 11 Pro trunk is a brushed cup, polished on

the rectangular camera. Notice, also, that the term "iPhone" has vanished once more from the back. I'm not implying that either iPhone 11 Pro is uncomfortable to carry; I'm especially keen on the brushed cup back on the iPhone 11 Pro max, which is on the rigid-still, somewhat torque-able-stainless steel framework - it feels good, appears razor-sharp, and hides your fingerprints completely. Apple's 6.1-inch iPhone 11, incidentally, features clean glass that still does a much better job of hiding fingerprints than the Gorilla Glass on the Samsung Galaxy Note 10+. Although the iPhone 11 Pro body isn't wildly the same as the iPhone XS but can sustain longer in water; the iPhone 11 Pro may survive thirty minutes in up to 4 meters of water.

I didn't have a deep pool open to me, but to ensure that the iPhone 11 Pro could deal with at least a dunk in the bathroom, I filled a cooler with about 2 ft of water and dropped both iPhone 11 Pro models; they easily survived ten minutes in the water.

iPhone 11 Pro submerged in water

Both the iPhone 11 and iPhone 11 Pro Potentially handled my water test like champs. Rather than wasting time wanting to persuade you that the iPhone 11 Pro camera module is much less unsightly as you believe that it is, I'd instead concentrate on the engineering feat it took to produce that raised package. The back is, in fact, one continuous bit of cup milled around the elevated square; it's a beautiful materials design down the cup circles encircling the three large lenses, and more significant True Firmness LED adobe flash and microphone openings. The cup will not cover the lens; instead, Apple is once more using Sapphire Crystal on all three, providing them with almost as much sapphire as you will probably find on the $749 Apple Watch face.

I love Apple's **Face ID** technology and its secure smart way to unlock, log in to online services, and make

obligations. But Apple's devotion to Face technology means that the TrueDepth module notch survives multiple iPhone decades even as competition is pressing everything off leading of their smartphones and only edge-to-edge and infinity displays. Others are drilling microscopic holes in their display screen to support selfie digital cameras (**OnePlus** put its selfie camera in a dangerous, mechanized pop-up camera component, leaving its display screen unblemished).

Apple states that Face Identification recognition is even faster than before. It is rapid and constant, but, at least in my assessments, not noticeably faster. I did so detect somewhat better off-angle face recognition.

I've now examined multiple Google android smartphones with an under-the-screen fingerprint sensor; while none of these is perfect, each of them works very well enough. To become reasonable to Apple, though, none of the competition ever built what I consider "near fool-proof face recognition technology."

iPhone 11 Pro and iPhone 11 Pro Max on Display Screen.

Apple's smartphones will have one of the very most noticeable dark bezels around their displays, at least in comparison with the *Samsung Galaxy Note 10+* and the *OnePlus 7 Pro*, both of which use curved displays to extend the edges of their screen visually.

There's also no iPhone 11 Pro or iPhone 11 Pro Max 5G option. Here, I believe Apple's made the right choice; 5G is a complicated and mostly non-existent clutter in the U.S. and probably won't suffice for another 12 months. At that time, Apple will have its 5G iPhone 12.

Screen Time

If we pass the figures, Apple's OLED Super Retina XDR screen is, at 458 ppi 2436x1125 pixels, not the sharpest smartphone screen on the marketplace. The 498 ppi Galaxy Notice 10+ keeps that honour; they are doing a match on the two 2,000,000:1 comparison ratio.

Apple's premiere smartphone now includes a Super Retina XDR screen. However, this a beautiful display screen, especially on the bigger device (2688x1242 pixels). The rise to 800 nits lighting (up to at least one 1,200 nits maximum) is incidentally noticeable entirely at daylight, at least when compared with the iPhone XS.

Perhaps the easiest way to see the display's stunning visual quality is by viewing 4K 60 FPS video. I shot some of the iPhone 11 Pro and was startled by the hyper-realism. Even on the tiny smartphone display. I've hardly ever really griped about the notch.

However, when a display is this good, it's a pity to devote the area to other things. The iPhone 11 Pro also marks the finish of 3D Touch; this under-the-screen technology held tabs on how hard you pressed on the display screen and would start additional, quick-access features on, say, the Camera application of the phone recognized more pressure as you kept your finger on the icon for a couple of seconds. The iPhone 11 Pro (as well as iPhone 11 Pro Max and standard 11 models) now use Haptic Touch exclusively, and you now have to press just a little much longer to access a few of these features and, in some instances, in specific places.

My thumb typing is abysmal, and I've relied on 3D Touch to press the keyboard display and gain fast access to the keyboard mouse, which let me split my finger around on the keyboard (as though it was on the trackpad), putting the cursor wherever I have to write. With Haptic Touch, I must press precisely on the area bar to trigger the digital trackpad (It's an annoyance that I'm already modifying to).

Camera Love for iPhone 11 Pro and iPhone 11 Pro Max

Whatever it is you like about the iPhone 11 Pro and 11 Pro Max camera design would fade when you begin using them. Nowadays, there are three 12 MP cameras at the back of the iPhone 11 Pro (apart from the size, all specs on the iPhone 11 Pro Max are similar, so my comments using one address both products).

Nowadays, there are four 12 MP digital cameras on these devices if you count number the main one in the TrueDepth component in front. There's the:

- *12 MP Wide (f/1.8 aperture)*

- *12 MP Ultra Wide (f/2.4 aperture with a 120-level field of view)*

- *12 MP Telephoto (f/2.0 aperture)*

Instantly, many of these lenses are bigger than those on the iPhone XS and XS Max; the brand new ultra-wide is a six-element lens, as the wide and telephoto are both five-element lenses.

A wide-angle view of that time Square

Most of them make excellent, colour-accurate, and detailed images. Apple is past due to the overall game with an ultra-wide zoom lens, but Apple brought its A-Game. Along with standard photos, you may use the ultra-wide zoom lens in the video, time-lapse (making them a lot more dramatic), and breathtaking, which creates an almost 360-level photo effect.

Capturing panorama photos in super-wide creates a near 360-level impact. Considering just how many selfies most of us take, getting the front-facing camera good (it's now 12 MP with an f/2.2 aperture) was a good move ahead of Apple's part.

I was impressed with the image quality, especially *family portrait mode*. With all the front-facing camera, you can also achieve a somewhat more wide position impact by tapping a set of arrow symbols on the display screen; this isn't a focus out or traditional wide position; instead, the camera is switching from hook crop of the entire 12 MP framework to a full-frame image, which enables you to pull more folks into the group selfie.

The very best part is that if you turn the camera to scenery orientation, the selfie camera automatically adjusts to full-frame. *The camera is also now with the capacity of shooting 4K 60 fps video, that I think is a boon for YouTubers who prefer to have the live-screen feedback while they shoot but hate sacrificing video quality (Now they can have both).*

It certainly nice when you're able to have a pro-level picture with one hand.

Just like the iPhone XR before it, the iPhone 11 Pro is now able to use the wide zoom lens to get more dramatic Family Portrait Mode images. The iPhone XS would combine both wide and telephoto, which design you always need to step back from your subject matter.

Camera Application Updated

To support each one of these new lens and photography options, Apple significantly updates its camera app.

iPhone 11 Pro Camera App

Rather than 1X and 2X and the primary zoom options, nowadays, there are three with ultra-wide, represented as a "0.5x" or fifty percent focus. It's choice I find just a little complication since Samsung describes its three capturing settings with a stand of trees and shrubs: one tree represents 2X, two represents no move, and a relatively distant band of three trees and shrubs represents ultra-wide (I honestly can't decide which is clearer).

Even if you're not in the iPhone 11 Pro's new ultra-wide camera mode, the new camera application will always demonstrate the amount of visual information you're abandoning: the dark borders of the camera application turn translucent, and that means you can see the actual ultra-wide zoom lens, which would be added if you were utilizing it.

Apple, also has introduced a Camera App drawer that you gain access to by swiping up close to the bottom level of the display. Under it, is aspect percentage *(4:3 or 16:9), Live photos, display screen, filters, HDR*, as well as your timer (I had been a little annoyed that Apple hid it this way). I love the new QuickTake video feature, which enables you to switch from picture set to video by just keeping down the shutter button. After that, you can slip it to lock it on while keeping the usage of a photo-in-video button on the right.

Probably the most exciting camera update, though, is *Night mode* (Apple's first feature-level effort with low-light photography). In this field, too, Apple is playing catch-up but with some rather stunning results.

Would you like to dance in the Pale Moonlight?
Night mode is not at all something you decide; instead, the iPhone 11 Pro automatically get on Night setting in low-light situations. It's indicated with a yellowish, eclipse-like icon in the top left-hand part of the Camera application screen.

Night mode comparison shot of the yellow bike in a shed

I took all three of the photos that was essentially a pitch dark shed; all three were able to catch a great deal of fine detail, but I believe Apple's Night setting gets the best balance of colour and clearness, Among the things I believe many people are surprised to find themselves using night time photo features on other mobile phones like Samsung's Galaxy collection and the Google Pixel; however, the dark requires the smartphone camera shutter to remain open for a couple of seconds and that you should stand still.

Night mode shot of the moon

In Nighttime mode, Apple offers a few of the most explicit help with ways to get the best ultra-low-light shot. I took photos in dark areas, enclosed almost lightless rooms, during the night; evening Setting instructed me to "Keep Still" as it modified the amount of time it would keep open up the shutter (usually, this between three and five seconds; you can view the shutter timer by gradually scrolling down). You can even either manually set the shutter to stay open up for 28 seconds to fully capture light paths or, if you place the smartphone on the tripod, allow the shutter to automatically opens up longer to fully capture.

iPhone 11 Pro Night shot with stars in the sky
Through a side-by-side-by-side test with the Google Pixel 3 and the Samsung Galaxy Notice 10+, Apple's iPhone 11 Pro Max produced the clearest Night mode shot. All three photos were good, but the Note10+ launched a lot of sound to the image and the Pixel 3 sacrificed some details for brightness.

Assessment of backlit selfie from iPhone 11 Pro and Galaxy Note 10+

I don't believe there's any question of 12 MP selfie camera doing a much better job here. The colours on the iPhone 11 Pro shot are accurate and, even in darkness, the facts on my face and throat are there. I did so, incidentally, switch off Samsung's default pores and skin filter to get the most accurate shot.

I'm also impressed with the changes Apple's designed to Smart HDR. Backlight photography is much better than what I possibly could achieve with my DSLR, which is without an adobe flash. In evaluations with Samsung's Galaxy Note 10+, the iPhone 11 Pro was able to accurately catch shadowed details lost or almost glossed over by rivals.

Self Family portrait in High-key Light Mono setting on iPhone 11 Pro

Apple, in addition, has improved the front-facing Portrait Setting photography algorithms. Despite having the new High Key mono setting, Apple was able to find the advantage of my bald mind and produce what appears to be studio-quality photos.

Capacity to Burn

You would believe that, right now, Qualcomm can achieve some parity with Apple, but Apple's bespoke silicon regularly stays a step before virtually all the mobile CPU manufacturers. Backed by, Geekbench, 3.68 GB of RAM, Apple's new A13 Bionic CPUs Geekbench 5 scores are significantly higher than those of the Qualcomm Snapdragon 855 mobile CPU.

Benchmarks

To place these quantities in framework, I played CPU-taxing video games like *Player Unknown's Battlegrounds and Asphalt 9*: Legends, and edited video, including 4K videos, on the iPhone 11 Pro with no issues. Asphalt, specifically, appeared amazing on the Super Retina XDR display screen.

Sound is going Spatial

The iPhone 11 Pro works just fine as a phone. Call

quality is clear, and the sound held up perfectly in stiff airflow. Music sounds great on the iPhone 11 Pro's stereo system speakers (the first at the bottom of these devices, the other is within the TrueDepth Component). Yes, it can get noisy, but what's fascinating is the new spatial audio.

iOS 13

The new iPhone 11 Pro (combined with the Pro Max and iPhone 11) comes with iOS 13. Apple's up-to-date mobile operating-system is filled with improvements, large and small. I've been running the beta on an iPhone XS for months and am still stumbling on new features and tiny adjustments.

Naturally, the mixture of iOS 13 and the latest iPhones is a perfect marriage. There will be the Camera mentioned above application updates, such as new portrait mode tools for adjusting essential light intensity, and they're paired with a completely new Photos app. Photos are currently a far more visually engaging native application that mixes in the image thumbnail sizes and includes video; it will pre-play videos. There's also the new *"For*

You Personally" tab that helpfully suggests shareable images. It's also where Apple collects your curated memories. It made a pleasant video out of all my Apple event images.

iPhone Home display in Dark Setting and improved Photos interface.

The much remaining is the iPhone home display screen in Dark Setting; next to it are two displays from the new Photos "*For You Personally*" tab, which got the long-awaited Dark Setting, and you can now quickly toggle it off by haptic-pressing the screen brightness control at the middle. I've never comprehended the obsession with Dark Mode, which means this is nice-to-have but, for me, at least, not-super-necessary upgrade.

Video Editing display on iPhone in iOS 13

I'm more impressed by the new local and non-destructive video editing tools, that are accessible through either the Camera application or in Photos. You've been able to cut videos and, with slow motion, change where the gradual effect starts and ends. You will adjust brightness, comparison, saturation, sharpness, sound decrease, and more. The best new indigenous video editing feature is cropping, which includes video styling, distortion, rotation, and flipping. There are a great number of third-party video applications that are going to get Sherlocked.

MAPS UPDATE

Apple also updated the Maps App, full disclosure: I take advantage of Apple maps on my iPhone at all times (the turn-by-turn directions I can get on my linked Apple Watch are priceless). iOS 13 provides real-time transit improvements (not that useful in NEW YORK where subway trains usually arrive every short while) and the powerful new *SHOP AROUND* feature.

Apple Maps SHOP AROUND street view

The look Around is nearly the same as Google's Road view, but with far better imagery. It isn't available almost everywhere, though. I came across good coverage for the *San Francisco Bay Area*, but none for *Manhattan*. Apple programs to move out more coverage by the end of the entire year.

In iOS 13, Siri's male and feminine voices do sound more natural, and I might begin using Siri Shortcuts, given that they're pre-installed in the iOS. I used the Shortcuts application to make a shortcut called "Distance to home," which, when I say, "Hey Siri, Distance to Home," would instantly calculate and show me what lengths it is from my current location to my home.

iOS 13 includes Plenty of Enhancements

There are a large number of other feature enhancements in iOS 13, including CarPlay Dashboard and the new Quick Path keyboard, which enables you to swipe across the virtual keyboard to type. I know many people love this feature on Android phones, but I could not get used to using it and still found typing the old-fashioned way faster and easier.

Apple, in addition, has added lots of new Animoji heroes, including an octopus and a cow. The best, though, will be the new Memoji Stickers, which combine common emoji expressions with your personal Animoji and that you can submit host to emojis via *iMessage, FaceTime*, and other apps. A few of iOS 13's better features, like Apple to Remain, where you may use your Apple ID to sign onto other applications and services, and advanced ARKit 3 tools like body tracking and individuals occlusion mostly await developers to introduce them in their apps. I did, however, see an early example of individuals occlusion in the Friends 25 app. It shows real potential.

Overall, I'd say this one of Apple's better OS updates. It manages to make significant system changes without somehow making the system unrecognizable.

Long Electric Battery Life

Unlike its smartphone competitors, Apple doesn't prefer to list the precise specifications of its iPhone batteries. So we're left with somewhat hazy guarantees like the iPhone 11 Pro *"continues 4 hours much longer than the iPhone XS"*, and the iPhone 11 Pro Maximum *"endures up to 5 hours much longer than the iPhone XS Max extent."* The truth is, I'd become more frustrated if these claims weren't right.

When I set up my new iPhone 11 Pro, I did so utilizing the backup from my previous iPhone; this intended the phone spending hours downloading old photos, videos, configurations, and apps, which wiped out your day One electric battery life. I attempted never to judge the phone too harshly because I've experienced this before with earlier new iPhones. By the next day, my iPhone 11 Pro was fully restored and, I didn't recharge it till the following morning; So, it's given me a day-plus about the same charge.

Indeed, I didn't do anything with the phone while I was sleeping, so we must slice out 9 hours of standby setting. So, let's say I acquired about 20 hours, and that is with turning Car Lock off and establishing screen lighting to near maximum. I did a similar thing, incidentally, with the top iPhone 11 Pro Max. As I write this, the iPhone 11 Pro has about 5% power staying and the iPhone 11 Pro Max has about 10%.

I did so not do anything special for doing that electric battery performance, but I also didn't, for example, play video gaming for 20-plus hours. I did so watch a two-hour movie at one point, but I also browsed the net, checked interpersonal media, took a lot of photos and video, paid attention to music, played games, and used several other apps. As always, your battery performance will change predicated on your own iPhone 11 Pro activities.

18W charger for new iPhone 11 Pro and Pro Max

Using the iPhone 11 Pro, Apple carries a redesigned charger for the very first time since switching to the lighting interface; this is Apple's first 18w fast charger for the iPhone; on one end of the included wire is the standard light charger that plugs into the bottom level of the iPhone, but on the other part is a USB-C plug and slot. Someday, I'm confident that Apple will change the iPhone to all USB-C. In a little more than an hour, the iPhone 11 Pro Max was nearly completely charged.

There's still wireless charging, which works efficiently with any Qi-based charger, but no wireless charge share. I was getting excited about putting my capable-of-charging-wirelessly AirPods 2 on the back of the iPhone 11 Pro, mainly because the phone now seems to have the juice to burn off. Apple has made a few changes to connection technology, including updating the Wi-fi to 802.11ax WiFi 6 and adding an Ultra-wideband (UWB) chip for spatial awareness. Eventually, you'll be able to immediate AirDrops by directing your iPhone at a particular recipient.

It's EXCELLENT

No more the thinnest, lightest, or even prettiest smartphone (it was never the least expensive), Apple appears prepared to rely increasingly more on people's devotion to the system (and its growing selection of services) and their desire to have excellent photography. The iPhone 11 Pro and much larger iPhone 11 Pro max are undoubtedly excellent smartphones, but they're built with an ageing chassis design that feels as though it's looking for an overhaul. Also, Apple made a blunder not starting the bottom models with 128 GB of storage space.

I don't expect one to choose the new iPhone since they want showing off their new camera square; however, they will upgrade for the new, formidable camera features.

Chapter 3

Comprehensive iPhone 11 Features

1. *Six New Gorgeous Colours*

The brand new iPhone 11 would come in six beautiful new colours; they're a little more in the pastel-colour range; however, they look quite right. The colours are *Crimson, White, Green, Yellowish, Dark, and Red.*

2. *Anodised Aluminium and 3D Cup Design*

As you can tell by looking at the back, the iPhone 11 has a fresh design at the end. The iPhone 11 shell is manufactured out of anodized aluminum, and on both edges, there's glass -panel. iPhone 11 includes a 3D cup design that seamlessly merges with the lightweight aluminum band.

3. *A13 Bionic Chip*

Apple says that the 7mm+ based *A13 Bionic chip* gets the fastest CPU in virtually any smartphone. It is up to 20% faster than the CPU inside the A12 chip. The A13 chip has special improvements for machine learning accelerators that permit the CPU to provide more than 1 trillion procedures per second.

4. *Fastest Smartphone GPU in the World*

Apple also says that the iPhone 11 gets the quickest GPU in virtually any smartphone in the marketplace. It's up to 20% faster than the GPU in iPhone XR while also being more power-efficient.

5. *New Main Camera*

The primary camera on the iPhone 11 has been updated; the 12MP sensor has 100% Concentrate Pixels for three times faster autofocus in low light.

6. *New Ultra Wide Camera*

The iPhone 11 gets an entirely new camera, and it's an ultra-wide sensor with a 120-level wide field of view; the 12MP Ultra Wide sensor has an f/2.4 aperture. It gives you to zoom out by 0.5x from the standard shot. By using this camera, you may take some fantastic cinematic shots with an entirely new perspective.

7. *4K Video on Ultra-Wide Camera*

The 4K recording works on the Ultra-Wide camera as well, and you may seamlessly switch between your cameras while shooting the video. You can tap on the move button to focus out, or you can split on the icon to slowly switch between your camera.

8. *Audio Zoom*

The Ultra-Wide camera and the new zoom technology includes an excellent addition in the program. As you move in and out of a video, the sound zooms too!

9. *Night Setting in Camera App*

iPhone 11 has a new low-light setting that converts on automatically and works with no flash. It requires multiple images, while optical image stabilization steadies the zoom lens. Then your software aligns the images with improving for movement and removes sections with too much blur. After that, it de-sounds and enhances all the available details. What you finish up with is your final image using which you can use as it is a lot brighter.

10. *QuickTake*

QuickTake is a fresh feature approaching later in the entire year that enables you to shoot videos while you're taking photos. What's incredible is that it'll keep carefully the same frame and everything the image settings, seamlessly switching to the video mode.

That is something that's not quick to do right now. After the feature boats, all you have to do is touch and hang on the Shutter button to begin recording a video. After that, you can swipe left to lock the video if you want to capture longer videos.

11. *12MP Front side Facing Camera*

There's a new and improved camera sensor in the TrueDepth camera system. It's now a 12MP sensor with an f/2.2 aperture.

12. *Faster Face Identification with Greater Angles*

Face ID is currently 30% faster, and it works at higher perspectives. So even if the telephone is in a roundabout way looking at you right in the facial skin, Face Identification unlock will still work.

13. *Slo-mo on Front side Facing Camera*

Apple wants to make selfies something. Now you can catch slow-motion video from the front-facing camera at up to 120 fps.

14. *4K Documenting on Front side Facing Camera*

Plus, you can record 4K video on the front-facing camera at 24, 30, or 60 fps.

15. *Portrait Setting Works together with Pets*

Thanks to the way the new wide and ultra-wide cameras interact, the portrait mode on the iPhone 11 now works for pets too! That is something we've wanted since Apple launched the iPhone XR this past year with Portrait mode but limited it only to humans.

16. *Spatial Sound with Dolby Atmos*

The speakers in the iPhone 11 include 3D Spatial sound technology. It simulates audio for a far more immersive experience; the brand new iPhone also comes with Dolby Atmos' support.

17. *Deep Fusion*

Deep Fusion is a new image control technology by Apple that will dispatch with a software update later in the Fall. It's another form of image structure technology. Apple requires four primary and four additional photos before you press the shutter button. When you press the shutter button, it requires one huge publicity picture to get as much fine detail as possible.

After that, it works pixel-by-pixel to stitch the facts collectively from all the photos in the best manner. Everything you get can be an image with an incredible level of detail.

18. *Longer Electric battery Life than iPhone XR*

iPhone XR already had a fantastic all-day electric battery life. iPhone 11 pushes the pub further with the addition of a complete hour to the electronic battery life. That's up to 17 hours of video playback or more to 10 hours of video loading time.

19. *New U1 Chip*

iPhone 11 has an entirely new chip called U1 that uses Ultra-Wideband technology for spacial consciousness; this enables iPhone 11 to locate other U1 devices precisely. If you wish to share a document using AirDrop, point your iPhone at theirs, and they'll be the first in the set of the AirDrop posting screen.

20. *Toughest Cup Ever in a Smartphone*

Apple has heard your issues loud and clear. Having a back again design that is accurately milled and sculpted from an individual piece of a cup, iPhone 11 features the most robust cup ever in a smartphone; this will help protect your iPhone in the event when it drops.

21. *Improved Water-Resistance*

iPhone 11 is IP68 certified; this implies it can withstand up to 2 meters of drinking water for thirty minutes.

22. *Extended Active Range*

The extended active range feature on the iPhone 11 while documenting videos is currently designed for 4k videos at up to 60fps. Around the iPhone XR, this is limited by

30fps videos only.

23. *Gigabit-class LTE*

iPhone 11 features Gigabit-class LTE that may help you get the best rates of speed on your moves; this is a significant omission on the iPhone XR, so it's nice to see Apple finally making your way around to adding it.

24. *Wi-Fi 6*

iPhone 11 is the first new iPhone to aid the new Wi-Fi 6 standard for faster download rates of speed. Apart from this, the iPhone 11 has yet featured that you found in iPhone XR. So that it still supports cellular charging, fast charging with the optionally available 18-watt charger that should be bought individually, Dual SIM support with eSIM, and more.

iPhone 11 will dispatch with iOS 13, with support for editing and enhancing 4K videos, dark setting, and many more.

Chapter 4

How to Customize Your iPhone Mobile

Customize iPhone Ringtones & Text message Tones

The ringtones and text tones your iPhone uses to get your attention need not be exactly like everyone else's. You may make all types of changes, including changing the tone, and that means you know who's phoning or texting without even taking a glance at your phone.

- *Change the Default Ringtone*: Your iPhone comes pre-loaded with a large number of ringtones. Change the default ringtone for all those calls to the main one you prefer the better to get notified when you experience a call to arrive. Do this by *heading to Settings -> Noises (Noises & Haptics on some models) -> Ringtone.*

- *Set Person Ringtones*: You can assign a different ringtone for everybody in your connections list. That way, a love track can play whenever your partner calls, and you know it's them before even looking. Do that by heading to *Phone -> Connections -> tapping the individual whose ringtone you want to improve -> Edit -> Ringtone.*

- **Get Full-Screen Photos for Incoming Phone calls**: The incoming call screen does not have to be boring. With this suggestion, you can view a fullscreen picture of the individual calling you. Go to *Mobile phone -> Connections -> touch the individual -> Edit -> Add Picture.*

- **Customize Text Tone**: Like everyone else can customize the ringtones that play for calls, you can customize the appearance like video when you get texts. Go to *Configurations -> Seems (Noises & Haptics on some models) -> Text message Tone.*

TIPS: You're not limited by the band and text tone that include the iPhone. You can purchase ringtones from Apple, and some applications help you create your tone.

Other iPhone Customization Options

Here's an assortment of a few of our other favorite ways to customize our iPhones.

- _**Delete Pre-Installed Apps**_: Got a couple of applications pre-installed on your iPhone you don't use? You can delete them (well, the majority of them, anyhow)! Just use the typical way to delete apps: Touch and keep until they tremble, then tap the x on the application icon.

- _**Customize Control Center**_: Control Center has a lot more options than are apparent initially. Customize Control Center to get just the group of tools you want to use. Head to _Settings -> Control Center -> Customize Settings._

- _**Install your preferred Keyboard**_: The iPhone includes an excellent onscreen keypad; nevertheless, you can install third-party keyboards that add cool features, like _Google search, emojis, and GIFs, plus much more._ Get yourself a new keyboard at the App Store, then go to _Settings ->_

General -> Keyboard -> Keyboards.

- **Make Siri a friend**: Choose to have Siri talk with you utilizing a man's tone of voice? It could happen. Head to *Settings -> Siri & Search -> Siri Tone of voice -> Male*. You can even go with different accents if you want.

- **Change Browser's default search engine**: Have search engines apart from Google that you'd like to use? Make it the default for those queries in Browser. Head to *Settings -> Browser -> Search Engine and making a fresh selection.*

- **Make Your Shortcuts**: If you an iPhone 11 or newer version user, you can create all sorts of cool customized gestures and shortcuts for various jobs.

- **Jailbreak Your Phone**: To obtain the most control over customizing your mobile phone, you can jailbreak it; this gets rid of Apple's settings over certain types of customization. Jailbreaking can cause functional problems and lessen your phone's security, but it can give more control.

Customize iPhone Home Screen

You may take a look at your iPhone home screen more than some other single screen so that it should be set up the way you want it to appear. Below are a few options for customizing your iPhone home screen.

- *Change Your Wallpaper*: You may make the image behind your applications on the home screen just about whatever you want. A favorite picture of your children or spouse or the logo design of your preferred team is a few options. Find the wallpaper settings by heading to *Settings -> Wallpaper -> Select a New Wallpaper*.

- *Use Live or Video Wallpaper*: Want something eye-catching? Use cartoon wallpapers instead. There are a few restrictions, but this is fairly cool. *Head to Settings -> Wallpaper -> Select a New Wallpaper -> pick and choose Active or Live*.

- *Put Apps into Folders*: Organize your home screen centred on how you utilize applications by grouping them into folders. Begin by gently tapping and securing one application until all your apps begin to tremble. Then pull and drop one application onto another to place those two applications into a folder.

- *Add Extra Webpages of Apps*: All your apps won't need to be about the same home screen. You may make individual "webpages" for different kinds of applications or different users by tapping and keeping applications or folders, then dragging them from the right side of the screen. Browse the *"Creating Web pages on iPhone"* portion of How to Manage Apps on the iPhone Home Screen to get more.

iPhone Customizations that make things Better to see

It isn't always a simple text message or onscreen items on your iPhone, but these customizations make things much simpler to see.

- *Use Screen Focus*: Do all the onscreen symbols

and text message look a little too small for your eye? Screen Move magnifies your iPhone screen automatically. To utilize this option, go to *Settings -> Screen & Brightness -> View -> Zoomed -> Collection.*

- **Change Font Size**: The default font size on your iPhone may be a little small for your eye; nevertheless, you can raise it to make reading convenient. Head to *Settings -> General -> Availability -> Larger Text message -> move the slider to On/green -> change the slider below.*

- **Use Dark mode**: If the shiny colors of the iPhone screen strain your eye, you may choose to use Dark Setting, which inverts shiny colors to darker ones. Find the essential Dark settings in *Configurations -> General -> Convenience -> Screen Accommodations -> Invert Colors.*

Customize iPhone Lock Screen

Like everyone else, you can customize your home screen; you can customize the iPhone lock screen, too. In this manner, you have control over the very first thing you see each time you wake up your phone.

- **_Customize Lock Screen Wallpaper_**: Exactly like on the home screen, you can transform your iPhone lock screen wallpaper to employ a picture, computer animation, or video. Browse the link within the last section for details.

- **_Create a Stronger Passcode_**: The much longer your passcode, the harder it is to break right into your iPhone (you are utilizing a passcode, right?). The default passcode is 4 or 6 character types (depending on your iOS version); nevertheless, you make it much longer and stronger. _Head to Settings -> Face ID (or Touch ID) & Passcode -> Change Passcode and following an instructions._

- **_Get Suggestions from Siri_**: Siri can learn your practices, preferences, passions, and location and then use that information to suggest content for you. Control what Siri suggests by heading to _Configurations -> Siri & Search -> Siri_

Recommendations and setting the things you want to use to On/green.

Customize iPhone Notifications

Your iPhone helpfully notifies you to understand when you have calls, text messages, emails, and other bits of information that may interest you. But those notifications can be irritating. Customize how you get notifications with these pointers.

- ***Choose Your Notification Style***: The iPhone enables you to choose lots of notification styles, from simple pop-ups to a mixture of sound and text messages, and more. Find the notification options in *Settings -> Notifications -> touch the application you want to regulate -> choose Alerts, Banner Style, Noises, and more.*

- ***Group Notifications from the Same App***: Get yourself many notifications from an individual app, but won't need to see each one taking space on your screen? You can group notifications into a *"stack"* that occupies the same space as your notification. Control this on the per-app basis by heading to *Settings -> Notifications -> the application you want to regulate -> Notification Grouping.*

- *Adobe flashes a Light for Notifications*: Unless you want to try out to get a notification, you may make the camera adobe flashlight instead. It's a delicate, but apparent, option for most situations. Set this up in *Settings -> General -> Convenience -> Hearing -> move the LED Screen for Notifications slider to On/green.*

- *Get Notification Previews with Face ID*: In case your iPhone has Face ID, you can utilize it to keep the notifications private. This establishing shows a simple headline in notifications; however, when you go through the screen and get identified by Face ID, the notification expands, showing more content. Establish this by going to *Settings -> Notifications -> Show Previews -> When Unlocked.*

TIPS: That link also offers an excellent tip about using Face ID to silent alarms, and notification sounds i.e., *"Reduce Alarm Volume and Keep Screen Shiny with Attention Awareness."*

- ***Get more information with Notification Center Widgets***: Notification Center not only gathers all your notifications, but it also offers up widgets, mini-versions of applications to enable you to do things without starting apps whatsoever.

Chapter 5

How to Create & Use iPhone 11 Shortcuts

How to Put in a Virtual Home Button to the iPhone

In respect to get a virtual Home button configured, you first have to allow the home button itself. Here's how:

- Touch *Settings*.

- Touch *General*.

- Touch *Accessibility*.

- Touch *AssistiveTouch*.

- Move the *AssistiveTouch* slider to On/green. The digital Home button shows up on your screen.

- Position the button anywhere on your screen using drag and drop.

- Make the button pretty much transparent utilizing the Idle Opacity slider.

- Touch the button to see its default menu.

How to Customize the Virtual Home Button Menu

To change the number of shortcuts and the precise ones that exist in the default menu:

- Around the *Assistive Touch* screen, tap Customize Top Level Menu.

- Change the number of icons shown in the very best Level Menu with the plus and minus control keys at the bottom of the screen. The minimum volume of options is 1; the utmost is 8. Each icon represents a different shortcut.

- To improve a shortcut, touch the icon you want to improve.

- Tap one of the available shortcuts from the list that appears.

- Touch Done to save the change. It replaces the shortcut you have chosen.

- If you decide you want to return to the default

group of options, touch Reset.

How to Add Custom Activities to the Virtual Home Button

Now that you understand how to include the virtual Home button and configure the menu, it is time to get to the nice stuff: custom shortcuts. As being a physical Home button, the digital button can be configured to react differently based on how you touch it. Some tips about what you must do:

Within the *AssistiveTouch* screen, go directly to the Custom Actions section. For that section, touch the action that you would like to use to result in the new shortcut. Your alternatives are:

- *Single-Touch*: The original single click of the home button. In cases like this, it's an individual touch on the digital button.

- *Double-Touch*: Two quick touches on the button; if you choose this, you can also control the Timeout establishing (i.e., the time allowed between touches) if additional time goes by between touches, the iPhone goodies them as two solitary touches, not a double-touch.

- **Long Press**: Touch and contain the virtual Home button. If you choose this, you can also configure a Duration, which sets how long you will need to press the screen because of this feature to be triggered.

- **3D Touch**: The 3D Touch screen on modern iPhones lets the screen respond differently based on how hard you press it. Utilize this option to have the digital Home button react to hard presses.

Whichever action you touch, each screen presents several options for shortcuts that you can assign to the action. They are especially cool because they change actions that may normally require pressing multiple control keys into an individual touch.

Most shortcuts are self-explanatory, such as Siri, Screenshot, or Volume Up, but a few need description:

- **Convenience Shortcut**: This shortcut may be used

to cause all types of convenience features, such as inverting colours for users with eyesight impairment, turning on VoiceOver, and zooming in on the screen.

- **Shaking**: Choose this, and the iPhone responds to a button touch as if an individual shook the telephone. Shake pays for undoing certain activities, particularly if physical issues prevent you from shaking the telephone.

- **Pinch**: Performs the same as a pinch gesture on the iPhone's screen, which pays for people who've impairments that produce pinching hard or impossible.

- **SOS**: This button allows the iPhone's Emergency SOS feature, which causes a loud sound to alert others that you might need help and a call to Emergency services.

- **Analytics**: This feature starts the gathering of Assistive Touch diagnostics.

Chapter 6

Top iPhone 11 Applications to Know

Spark: Best Email App for iPhone 11

If you centre on iOS apps, you would understand that email has taken on something similar to the role of the antagonist in the wonderful world of iOS. App designers appear to know that everyone needs a better email platform, and they want an application to resolve their issues. Controlling email is just a little less stressful if you are using *Spark* as you would find features to suit your needs, such as; sending, snoozing email messages, and a good inbox that only notifies you of important email messages.

Below are the things you'd like about this application:

- The app is simple to use and socially friendly.

- Swipe-based interaction allows for one-handed operation.

What You may not like about it:

- No filter systems for automatically sorting email messages.

- The app does not have a way of controlling messages in batches.

Things: The best "To-do manager" for the iPhone 11

To-do manager applications are a packed field, and the application called *"Things"* isn't the only good one, and it is also not the only *to-do manager* on this list, but it's a carefully reliable tool, seated between control and hardy. The application provides the ideal levels of both control and hardy, without mind-boggling users to dials and without dropping essential features.

Things you'd like about this application:

- This app has a simplified interface that reduces stress when adding and completing the task.

- Tasks can be added from iOS with the sheet extension.

What you may not like are:

- Repeating tasks and deadlines can be buggy.

- Tasks can't be put into the calendar automatically.

OmniCentre: Best GTD-compatible To-Do App for iPhone 11

Like *"Things,"* **OmniCentre** is a favourite and well-designed to-do manager; however, they have a different group of priorities. Where **Things** attempts to remain simple and straightforward, **OmniCentre** is feature-rich and robust.

The application fully integrates with the **"Getting Things Done"** approach to task management called **GTD**, and this method stimulates users to jot down any duties they have, as well as almost all their associated information and scheduling. GTD users would finish up spending a great deal of time on leading end arranging work; because of this, the software takes a robust feature collection to implement all areas of the GTD process.

Things you'd like about this application:

- Most effective to-do list manager available.

- Can participate in virtually any task management style.

What you may not like:

- Sacrifices simpleness and usability for power and versatility.

Agenda: Best iPhone 11 App for Busy Notice Takers

Agenda requires a different spin on the notes application than almost every other application; its also known as *"date centred notice taking app."* Records are structured by task and day, and the times are a large part of the Agenda. Instead of merely collecting your jotting into a collection, Agenda creates a to-do list from *"things,"* with tight time integration, Agenda makes an operating journaling app and an able to-do manager and general iPhone 11 note-taking app. The day and note mixture seems apparent, but Agenda is the first iOS note-taking application to perform this mixture effectively.

It's a "to-do manager" and also a note-taking application with some calendar features, which enables seeing every information in a single place with one perspective and only one app. The application is also highly practical in the freeform, which may be uncommon in flagship apps. The beauty of the app *"Agenda"* comes out when using Pencil support, but for the present time, we'll have to turn to the iPad Pro for the feature.

Things you'd like about this application:

- Note-taking small tweaks can improve many workflows.

- The time-based organization fits most users; mental types of information organization.

What you may not like:

- Slow app release can limit how quickly you can write down a note.

1Password: Best iPhone 11 App for Security password Management

Using the auto-fill in iOS 13, *1Password* is as near to perfect as we have in a password manager. The Face ID authentication isn't unique to the iPhone 11 alone, but access Face ID makes the application better and simpler to use, which is an uncommon combination of accomplishments to reach concurrently.

Things you'd like about this application:

- Finding and copying usernames and passwords is extremely easy.

- Secure document storage space means *1Password* can gather all of your secure information in a single place.

- Auto-fill support finally makes security password management as easy as typing your security password.

What you may not like:

- No free version.

- The paid version uses membership pricing.

Twitterific: Best Tweets App For iPhone 11

Twitter is probably not the most exceptional sociable media system, but it's still one of the very most popular internet sites around, and like many internet sites, Twitter's default application is disappointingly bad.

Unfortunately, Twitter does lately nerf third-party Twitter clients. Third-party applications won't receive real-time stream notifications, significantly reducing the effectiveness of the applications; this move seems to pressure users to go to the native app, but considering its many defects, Twitterific and applications like it remain better.

Things you'd like about this application:

- Improves Twitter's visual demonstration dramatically.

- Includes smart and powerful features that make Twitter simpler to use.

What you may not like:

- Some organizational options are initially unintuitive.

- Twitter has purposefully knee-capped a good number of third-party apps, and Twitterific is no defence to those results.

<u>Overcast</u>: *Best iPhone 11 App for Podcasts*

Overcast is the best application you may use to hear podcasts. The app's user interface is considered carefully for maximal consumer performance, with features like "Smart Rate" which helps to intelligently manages a podcast's playback speed to shorten silences without accelerating speech, while Tone of voice Boost offers a pre-built EQ curve made to amplify voices, which is ideal for a loud hearing environment.

Things you'd like about this application:

- Thoughtfully designed interface for sorting and hearing podcasts.

- Features like Smart Speed and Queue playlists are invaluable once you're used to them.

- Active developer centred on avoiding an unhealthy user experience concerning monetization.

What you may not like;

- It most definitely doesn't seem to go nicely with the iOS lock screen.

<u>Apollo</u>: Best iPhone 11 App for Reddit

If you're thinking about *Reddit*, you would want to see the website beyond the third-party app. The application has improved, sure, but it's still kilometres behind third-party offerings.

Apollo is the best of the number as it pertains to Reddit clients, conquering out past champions like "Narwhal." Development is continuous and ongoing, with many improvements from the dev in the app's subreddit.

The swipe-based navigation would continue to work on any iPhone, of course, but it dovetails nicely with the iPhone 11's application switching behaviour. The real black setting is also a delicacy for OLED screens.

Things you'd like about this application:

- Effortlessly handles an enormous variety of media.

- Well developed UI makes navigation easy.

- No ads in virtually any version of the app.

What you may not like:

- Sometimes is suffering from annoying and lingering bugs.

Focos: Best iPhone 11 App for Editing and enhancing Portrait Setting Photos

By default, the iPhone 11's Family portrait Mode is a one-and-done process; you take the picture, and the blur is applied. iOS doesn't give a built-in way for editing and enhancing the Picture Setting effect following the fact. Focos fills the space, creating a tool to tweak both degrees of shadow and the blur face mask. It mimics the result you'd see when modifying a zoom lens' physical aperture. More magically, you can also change the centre point following the shot by recreating the blurred cover up on the different object, or by hand adjusting the result on the image's depth face mask instantly.

Things you'd like about this application:

- The most effective approach to manipulating Portrait Mode's depth-of-field effect.

- The depth map is a distinctive feature to help visualize blur.

What you may not like:

- Simple to make images look over-processed.

- Only about the centre, 50% of the blur range looks natural.

Halide: Best iPhone 11 App for Natural Photos

Distinctively, *Halide* sticks essential info in the iPhone 11's "ear." It embeds a live histogram for image evaluation; could it be precious? Nearly, but Halide is a near-perfect picture taking software besides that offering feature.

The settings are ideally positioned and configured, the RAW catch is pixel-perfect, and navigation within the application is easy and immediately understandable. If you are seriously interested in taking photos on your iPhone 11, *Halide* is the best camera application for iOS.

Things you'd like about this application:

- Low handling power for iPhone photos.

- The broadest toolset of any iOS image editing and enhancing the app.

What you may not like:

- It can overwhelm first-time users using its degree of control.

Euclidean Lands: The Top-rated AR Puzzle Game for iPhone 11

Augmented reality applications haven't yet found their killer use. But AR gambling takes great benefit from lots of the iPhone 11's features.

Euclidean Lands is a short fun puzzler that calls for the full benefit of AR's potential. Similar to Monument Valley, players manipulate the play space to produce new pathways through puzzle designs, guiding their avatar to the finish of the maze. The overall game begins easy; nevertheless, you might be scratching your head just a little by the end.

Things you'd like in this application:

- Challenging and attractive puzzle levels that take benefit of AR's unique features.

What you may not like:

- Disappointingly short.

- The core game auto technician feels very familiar.

Giphy World: Best AR Messaging App for iPhone 11

Plenty of applications have tried to usurp Snapchat as an AR messaging system. While Snapchat might maintain a weakened condition because of self-inflicted damage, it isn't eliminated yet. But if it can decrease, Giphy World is a great replacement.

Things you'd like about this application:

- Simple to create fun and funny images from provided assets.

- Content isn't locked inside the Giphy app.

What you may not like:

- Object place and processing speed are inferior compared to Snapchat's.

Jig Space: Best Usage of AR for Education on iPhone 11

Learning with holograms is one particular thing you regularly see in sci-fi movies; with *Jig Space* and *augmented* actuality, that kind of thing is now possible in our daily lives. You should use the application to find out about various topics, including what sort of lock works, manipulating every part of the system, and looking at it from alternative perspectives. Jig Space requires the benefit of AR's three sizes effectively, and the low-poly models AR has bound not to harm the grade of the visualizations.

Things you'd like about this application:

- Takes benefit of AR's advantages for a good cause.

- A substantial assortment of "jigs" charges is free.

What you may not like:

- Accompanying captions are occasionally disappointingly shallow.

Nighttime Sky: Best Late-Night Outside Companion App

Directing out constellations is much more fun if you are

not making them up as you decide to go. *Evening Sky* was the main augmented-reality style application to seem on iOS. It shows just how for others on the system wanting to mimic its success, but it's remained dominant nevertheless.

Things you'd like about this application:

- It enhances the natural world with technology.

- It improves the star-gazing experience for both children and adults.

What you may not like:

- Large image units mean large camera motions are stiff and jerky.

<u>Inkhunter</u>: *Most Readily Useful AR Gimmick on iOS*

There's something distinctively exotic about checking out new tattoos by yourself. *Inkhunter* uses the energy of augmented truth to generate short-term digital symbols you can construct on the body and screenshot. You should use the built-in adobe flash, pull your designs, or import property from somewhere else to project on your skin.

Things you'd like about this application:

- Fun and book application idea that's useful.

What you may not like:

- Is suffering from AR's existing restrictions in surface matching.

Chapter 7

iPhone 11 Gestures You Should Know

Just like the iPhone 7 launched in 2017, the iPhone 11 doesn't include a physical home button, instead deciding on gestures to regulate the new user interface. It would require a couple of days to get used to the change but stay with it. By day three, you'll question how you ever coped without it, and using an "old" iPhone would appear old and antiquated.

1. **Unlock your iPhone 11:** Go through the phone and swipe up from underneath the screen. It truly is that easy, and also you don't need to hold back for the padlock icon at the very top to improve to the unlock visual before swiping up.

2. **Touch to wake:** Tap on your iPhone 11 screen when it's off to wake it up and find out what notifications you have. To unlock it with FaceID, you'll still have to set it up.

3. **Back to the Homescreen:** Whatever application you are in, if you would like to return to the Home screen, swipe up from underneath of the screen. If you're within an application that is operating scenery, you'll need to keep in mind slipping up from underneath the screen (i.e., the medial side) rather than where the Home button used to be.

4. **Have a screenshot:** Press the power button and the volume up button together quickly, and it would snap a screenshot of whatever is on the screen.

5. **Addressing Control Centre:** It used to be always a swipe up, now it's a swipe down from the very best right of the screen. Even if your iPhone doesn't have 3D Touch, you can still long-press on the symbols to gain usage of further configurations within each icon.

6. **Accessing open up apps:** Previously, you raise tapped on the home button to uncover what apps you'd open. You now swipe up and then pause with your finger on the screen. After that, you can

see the applications you have opened up in the order you opened them.

7. **Launch Siri**: When you may use the "Hey Siri" hot term to awaken Apple's digital associate, there are still ways to release the function utilizing a button press. Press and contain the wake/rest button on the right aspect of the phone before Siri interface pops-up on screen.

8. **Switch your phone off**: Because long-pressing the wake/rest button launches Siri now, there's a fresh way for switching the phone off. To take action, you would need to press and contain the wake/rest button and the volume down button at the same time. Now glide to power off.

9. **Release Apple Pay**: Again, the wake/rest button is the main element here. Double touch it, and it would talk about your Apple Budget, then scan that person, and it'll request you to keep your phone near to the payment machine.

10. **Gain access to widgets on the lock screen**: Swipe

from still left to directly on your lock screen, ideal for checking your activity bands.

Using Memoji

- **Create your Memoji**: Open up Messages and begin a new meaning. Touch the tiny monkey icon above the keypad, and then strike the "+" button to generate your personality. You would customize face form, skin tone, curly hair colour, eye, jewellery, plus much more.

- **Use your Memoji/Animoji in a FaceTime call**: Take up a FaceTime call, then press the tiny star icon underneath the corner. Now, tap the Memoji you want to use.

- **Memoji your selfies**: So, if you select your Memoji face, preferably to your real to life face, you can send selfies with the Memoji changing your head in Messages. Take up a new message and touch the camera icon, and then press that top button. Now choose the Animoji option by tapping that monkey's mind again. Choose your Memoji and tap the '*X*,' not the "done" button, and then take your picture.

- **Record a Memoji video:** Sadly, Memoji isn't available as a choice in the camera app, but that doesn't mean you can't record one. Much like the picture selfie, go to communications, touch on the camera icon and then slip to video and then tap on the superstar. Weight the Animoji or your Memoji, and off you decide to go.

iOS 13 iPhone 11 Notification Tips

- *Notifications collection to provide quietly*: If you're worried that you would be getting way too many notifications, you can place the way they deliver with an app by application basis. Swipe left when you've got a notification on the Lock screen and touch on Manage. Touch Deliver Quietly. Calm notifications come in Notification Centre, but do not show up on the Lock screen, play audio, present a banner or badge the application icon. You've just surely got to be sure you check every once in a while.

- *Switch off notifications from an app*: Same method as the "Deliver Quietly" feature, other than you tap the "Switch off..." option.

- *Open up Notification Centre on Lock screen*: From your lock screen, swipe up from the center of the screen, and you would visit a long set of earlier notifications if you have any.

- *Check Notifications anytime*: To check on your Notifications anytime, swipe down from the very best left part of the screen to reveal them.

Using Screen Time

- *Checking your Screen Time*: You can examine how you've been making use of your phone with the new Screen Time feature in iOS 13. You'll find the reviews in *Configurations > Screen Time.*

- *Scheduled Downtime:* If you want just a little help making use of your mobile phone less, you can restrict what applications you utilize when. Check out Settings > Screen Time and choose the Downtime option. Toggle the change to the "on" position and choose to routine a period when only specific applications and calls are allowed. It's ideal for preventing you or your children from using their cell phones after an arranged time, for example.

- **Set application limits**: App Limitations enable you to choose which group of applications you want to include a period limit to. Choose the category and then "add" before choosing a period limit and striking "plans."

- **Choose "always allowed" apps**: However, you might be willing to lock down your phone to avoid you utilizing it, that's no good if most of your way of getting in touch with people is via an application that gets locked away. Utilize this feature always to allow certain applications whatever limitations you apply.

- **Content & Personal privacy limitations**: This

section is also within the primary Screen Time configurations menu and particularly useful if you are a mother or father with kids who use iOS devices. Utilizing it, you can restrict all types of content and options, including iTunes and in-app buys, location services, advertising, etc. It's worth looking at.

Siri shortcuts

- *Siri Shortcuts*: There are several little "help" the iPhone 11 offers via Siri Shortcuts. To start to see the ones recommended for you, go to *Configurations > Siri & Search* and choose what you think would be helpful from the automatically produced suggestions. Touch "all shortcuts" to see more. If you wish to install specific "shortcuts" for a variety of different applications that aren't recommended by the iPhone, you can do this by downloading the dedicated Siri Shortcuts.

iPhone 11 Control Centre Tips

- *Add new handles*: Just like the previous version of iOS, you can include and remove handles from Control Centre. Check out *Configurations > Control Centre > Customize Handles* and then choose which settings you would like to add.

- *Reorganize handles*: To improve the order of these settings, you've added, touch, and contain the three-bar menu on the right of whichever control you would like to move, then move it along the list to wherever you would like it to be.

- *Expand handles*: Some settings may become full screen, press harder on the control you want to expand, and it will fill the screen.

- *Activate screen recording*: Among the new options, you can include regulating Centre is Screen Recording. Be sure you add the control, then open up Control Centre and press the icon that appears like an excellent white circle in the thin white band. To any extent further, it'll record everything that occurs on your screen. Press the control again if you are done, and it will save a video to your Photos application automatically.

- *Adjust light/screen brightness*: You can activate your camera adobe flash, utilizing it as a torch by starting Control Centre and tapping on the torch icon. If you wish to adjust the lighting, power press the icon, then adapt the full-screen slider that shows up.

- *Quickly switch where a sound is played*: One cool feature is the capability to change where music is playing. While music is playing, through Apple Music, Spotify, or wherever, press on the music control or touch the tiny icon in the very best part of the music control; this introduces a pop-up screening available devices that you can play through; this may be linked earphones, a Bluetooth loudspeaker, Apple Television, your iPhone, or any AirPlay device.

- *Set an instant timer*: Rather than going to the timer app, you can force press on the timer icon, then glide up or down on the full-screen to create a timer from about a minute to two hours long.

- *How to gain access to HomeKit devices*: Open up Control Centre and then tap on the tiny icon that appears like a home.

iPhone 11 Photos and Camera Tips

- *Enable/disable Smart HDR*: Among the new iPhone's camera advancements is HDR, which helps boost colors, light, and detail in hard light conditions. It's on by default, but if you would like to get it turned on or off, you manually can check out *Settings > Camera and discover the Smart HDR toggle change.*

- *Keep a standard photograph with HDR*: Right under the Smart HDR toggle is a "Keep Normal Photo" option, which would save a regular, no HDR version of your picture as well as the Smart HDR photo.

- **Portrait Lights**: To take Portrait Setting shots with artificial lights, first go to capture in Family portrait mode. Portrait Setting only works for people on the iPhone 11 when capturing with the rear-facing camera. To choose your Portrait Setting capturing style, press and hang on the screen where it says "DAYLIGHT" and then move your finger to the right.

- **Edit Portrait Lights after taking pictures**: Open up any Family portrait shot in Photos and then tap "edit." After another or two, you will see the light effect icon at the bottom of the image, touch it, and swipe just as you did when shooting the picture.

- **Edit Portrait setting Depth**: Using the new iPhone 11, you can modify the blur impact after shooting the Portrait shot. Check out Photos and choose the picture you want to regulate, then select "edit." You will see a depth slider at the bottom of the screen. Swipe to boost the blur strength, swipe left to diminish it.

- **How exactly to Merge People in Photos app**:

Photos in iOS can check out your photos and identify people and places. If you discover that the application has chosen the same person, but says they vary, you can combine the albums collectively. To get this done, go directly to the Photos application > Albums and choose People & Places. Touch on the term "Select" at the very top right of the screen and then select the images of individuals you want to merge, then tap "merge."

- *Remove people in Photos app*: Head to Photos App, Albums, and choose People & Places. To eliminate tap on "Choose" and then tap on individuals, you do not want to see before tapping on "Remove" underneath still left of your iPhone screen.

iPhone 11: Keyboard Tips

- *Go one-handed*: iOS 13's QuickType keypad enables you to type one-handed, which is fantastic on the larger devices like the iPhone 11 and XS Greatest extent. Press and contain the emoji or world icon and then keypad configurations. Select either the still left or right-sided keypad. It shrinks the keyboard and techniques it to 1 aspect of the screen. Get back to full size by tapping the tiny arrow.

- *Use your keyboard as a trackpad*: Previously, with 3D Touch shows, you utilize the keyboard area as a trackpad to go the cursor on the screen. You'll still can, but it works just a little in a different way here, rather than pressure pressing anywhere on the keypad, press, and hangs on the spacebar instead.

Face ID Tips

- ***Adding another in-person ID***: if you regularly change appearance now, you can put in a second In person ID to state the iPhone 11 getting puzzled. That is also really useful if you would like to add your lover to allow them to use your mobile phone while you're traveling, for example.

iPhone 11: Screen Tips

- ***Standard or Zoomed screen***: Since iPhone 6 Plus, you've had the opportunity to select from two quality options. You can transform the screen settings from Standard or Zoomed on the iPhone 11 too. To change between your two - if you have changed your mind after set up - go to *Configurations > Screen & Lighting > Screen Focus and choose Standard or Zoomed.*

- ***Enable True Tone screen***: If you didn't get it done

at the step, you could transform it anytime. To get the iPhone's screen to automatically change its color balance and heat to complement the background light in the area, check out Control Centre and push press the screen lighting slider. Now touch the True Firmness button. You can even go to *Configurations > Screen and Lighting and toggle the "True Shade" switch.*

iPhone 11 Battery Tips

- **Check your average battery consumption**: In iOS 13, you can check out Settings > Battery, and you will see two graphs. One shows the electric battery level; the other shows your screen on and screen off activity. You would find two tabs. One shows your last day; the other turns up to fourteen days; this way, you can view how energetic your phone battery strength and breakdowns screening your average screen on and off times show under the graphs.

- **Enable Low-Power Mode**: The reduced Power

Mode (Settings > Electric battery) enables you to reduce power consumption. The feature disables or lessens background application refresh, auto-downloads, email fetch, and more (when allowed). You can turn it on at any point, or you are prompted to carefully turn it on at the 20 and 10 % notification markers. You can even put in control to regulate Centre and get access to it quickly by swiping up to gain access to Control Centre and tapping on the electric battery icon.

- *Find electric battery guzzling apps*: iOS specifically lets you know which apps are employing the most power. Head to Configurations > Electric battery and then scroll right down to the section that provides you with an in-depth look at all of your battery-guzzling apps.

- *Check your battery via the Electric battery widget*: Inside the widgets in Today's view, some cards enable you to start to see the battery life staying in your iPhone, Apple Watch, and linked headphones. Just swipe from left to directly on your Home screen to access your Today view and scroll until you start to see the "Batteries" widget.

- *Charge wirelessly*: To utilize the iPhone's wifi charging capabilities, buy a radio charger. Any Qi charger will continue to work, but to charge more effectively, you will need one optimized for Apple's 7.5W charging.

- *Fast charge it*: When you have a 29W, 61W, or 87W USB Type-C power adapter for a MacBook, you can plug in your iPhone 11 Pro utilizing a Type-C to Lightning wire watching it charge quickly. Up to 50 % in thirty minutes.

Chapter 8

iPhone 11 Guidelines: How to unlock its Photographic Potential

Taking photos in the iPhone's default camera application is pretty simple and straightforward - in fact, almost too simple for individuals who need to get a little more creative using their shots. Well, that's all transformed on the iPhone 11 and iPhone 11 Pro, which not only brings a fresh wide-angle zoom lens but a pleasant assisting of new software features that you should explore.

The difficulty is, a few of these aren't immediately apparent, and it's not necessarily clear just how to take benefit of the excess photographic power stored in your shiny new iPhone.

That's why we've come up with this beginner guide for the iPhone 11 and iPhone 11 Pro's digital cameras, to get a solid foothold and springtime towards Instagram greatness. Continue reading and get snapping.

1. *Figure out how to look beyond your frame*

When shooting the typical (26mm comparative) zoom lens, the iPhone 11 and iPhone 11 Pro use the wide-angle zoom lens showing you what's happening beyond your frame, a little just like a range-finder camera. Those digital cameras have always been popular with professional road photographers because they enable you to nail the precise moment when a fascinating character walks into the frame.

You shouldn't do anything to create this up - endure your iPhone 11 with the camera application open and point it towards the scene to view it in action. Look for a photogenic background like a vacant road, then use the wide-angle preview to time as soon as your subject matter enters the shot. Want to keep the wide-angle view of your picture carefully.

2. *Adjust your compositions*

Here's another fun new feature on the iPhone 11 and iPhone 11 Pro that's great if you can't quite determine the ultimate way to take a picture. You'll need to go to the main configurations, wherein the Camera section; you'll find an option called *"Composition."* If you enable "Photos Catch Outside the Framework," the camera will record two photos at the same time - one using the wide-angle zoom lens, and another using the typical angle.

There are always a few facts to consider when working with this nifty trick. First is that you'll have to take in the HEIF format, which isn't always dealt with well by non-iOS devices. Also, the broader position picture will be erased if it's not used within thirty days, so you'll have to be reasonably quick with your editing and enhancing.

To get the wide-angle view of the shot, tap *'Edit'* within the photo, then your cropping icon, then press the three dots button in the very best right and choose "Use Content Beyond your Frame."

3. *Manage HDR*

The iPhone 11 and iPhone 11 Pro include Smart HDR, which is started up by default; this automatically detects the light levels in your picture and protect both shows and shadows for a far more balanced image.

More often than not, you will see occasions when challenging conditions lead to a graphic, which is nearly right. If you'd favour less processed photos to edit within an application like Lightroom, check out the configurations menu, find the Camera section, then switch off Smart HDR.

The great thing concerning this is it doesn't eliminate using Smart HDR for several scenes - in the Camera application, you'll now see an HDR button at the very top to turn it On/Off. It just means your default capturing will be without Smart HDR's sometimes overzealous processing.

4. _Reach grips with Night Mode_

Night mode is a new feature for the iPhone 11 and iPhone 11 Pro - and it's something we've been waiting around to see in a while. It's not an ardent setting you can opt for - instead, it'll activate automatically when the iPhone detects that ambient light conditions are on the reduced side.

Nevertheless, you can still have little control over it once it is used; tap the night time setting icon at the left, and you may use a split to choose a faster shutter speed if it's brighter than the telephone realizes, or leave it on Car - or you can also choose to turn it off entirely carefully.

It's worth keeping your iPhone 11 constant on the surface, or perhaps a tripod if you have one, as the telephone will recognize this and raise the shutter rate to 30 mere seconds, which is potentially ideal for night sky photos.

5. _Grasp the ultra-wide-angle lens_

The iPhone 11 and iPhone 11 Pro will be the first ones with a super wide-angle lens. If you haven't used one before, their 13mm equivalent field of view will come in super-handy for several different subjects, but particularly landscape and architecture, where you want to fit in as much of the scene as possible.

If you wish to exceed dramatic building pictures, one common technique utilized by professional scenery photographers is to juxtapose one close object with a distant object - for example, some close by plants with a long way background subject.

You could also want to use it in a while composing in portrait orientation, for a fascinating new look that wouldn't have been possible before with older iPhones.

6. *Portrait setting is not only for humans*

Even though iPhone XR had a great camera, you couldn't use the inbuilt Family portrait mode for anything apart from human subjects. Bad information for pet-lovers, or merely those who wish to create a shallow depth of field results with any subject.

That's all transformed for the iPhone 11, which uses its two digital cameras to help you to take shallow depth-of-field impact images for many different subjects, and has been specially optimised for domestic pets. To begin with, all you have to do is swipe to *Family portrait mode* and point the camera the four-legged friend. It'll tell you if you're too near to the subject and instruct you to move away. The details are nearly perfect, but they're perfect - particularly if you're looking on a little screen.

7. *Locate those lacking settings*

Through the keynote release of the iPhone 11 and iPhone 11 Pro, it was announced that the native camera application would be simplified to help you consider the key method of shooting your images.

That's great and produces a much cleaner interface, but it can imply that some configurations are now just a little concealed away. If you think where they've eliminated, touch the arrow near the top of the display, and you'll find a range of different alternatives, including aspect percentage (see below), adobe flash, night setting (if it's dark enough), timer and digital filter systems.

8. *Try the new 16:9 aspect ratio*

This is an attribute that is new for the iPhone 11 and

iPhone 11 Pro, adding a new aspect ratio to the prevailing 4:3 and square (1:1) options. Using a 16:9 aspect percentage is ways to get more full shots which ingest more of the scene, and also eventually screen very nicely on the iPhone display screen.

You'll need to activate it from the menu - the default is 4:3. It's well worth also using the 16:9 aspect proportion with the ultra-wide position to get some good great breathtaking type shots.

Chapter 9

How to start Dark Setting on your iPhone in iOS 13

First, check out *'Configurations'* and then look for *'Screen & Lighting.'* Once there, you'll see an all-new interface that places dark setting front side and centre. You will toggle between *'Light'* and *'Dark'* mode with only a tap, assuming you want to activate it manually; however, its implementation within iOS is just a little smarter than either 'on' or 'off.'

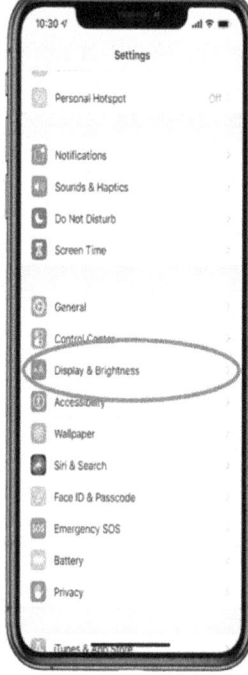
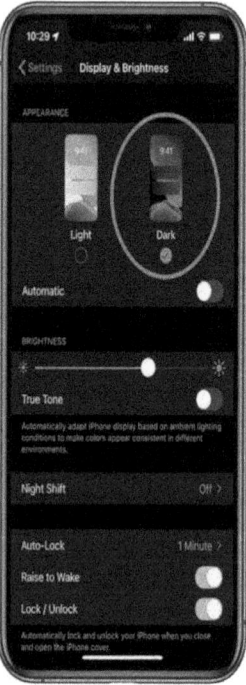

Under the two main options, you'll also visit a toggle marked *'Automatic'* which, as you may be able to think, switches dark setting on alone, linked with sunset and sunrise. Additionally, you then have the choice to define specific times for dark settings to allow and disable.

Dark mode has shown to be one of the very most hyped features approaching to cellular devices in 2019. It isn't just a capability destined for iOS 13 either, it's a significant feature in Google android ten plus some devices have previously instigated their own undertake dark setting - cell phones like the Asus ZenFone 6 and the OnePlus 7 Pro.

What does Dark Mode in iOS 13 do?

A part of dark mode's charm originates from the decrease in power usage it brings, particularly on devices that use OLED shows, like the iPhone X, XS, and XS Maximum. Beyond power intake, however, darker interface shades also lessen eye strain, particularly when being viewed in dark surroundings. In some cases, alternative UI and font colours are also associated with alleviating conditions like Scotopic Level of sensitivity Syndrome - an affliction commonly within people that have dyslexia, which makes text visibility and comprehension difficult.

How to Upgrade Applications on your iPhone in iOS 13

If you're used to manually updating your applications on either an iPhone, iPad or iPod touch by going to the updates tabs in the App Store, then iOS 13 has made some changes. That tabs has eliminated and has been changed by *Arcade*. If you don't anticipate using the new Apple Arcade membership video gaming service, then there's no chance to eliminate this.

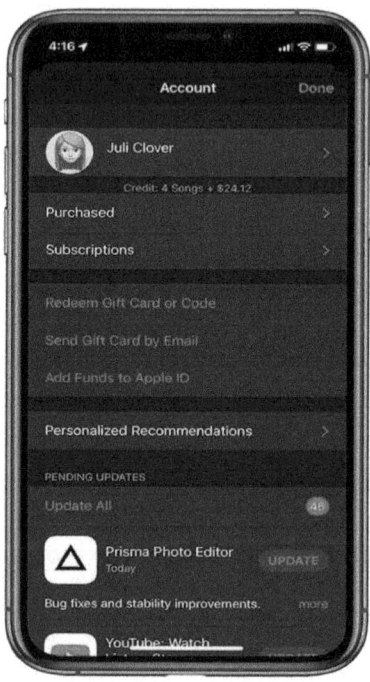

He

- Start the App Store on your iPhone.

- Tap the round consumer icon at the right-hand corner.

- Scroll down, and you'll see a list of all of your applications that either have updates available or have been recently updated.

- If an application comes with an update available, you can hit the button to start it manually.

Do applications automatically upgrade in iOS 13?

It appears clear that the reason behind Apple moving this program is because applications tend to update themselves quietly in the background, removing the necessity for anybody to manage application updates manually. The downside with this is that it could be challenging to learn what new features have found its way to applications if you're not looking at the release notes.

Chapter 10

5 Differences Between iPhone 11 & iPhone X

Apple enthusiasts unite: Many long-anticipated Apple announcements were confirmed and unveiled throughout a live blast of the Apple event that was hosted by Apple CEO **Tim** at the Steve Careers Theater on Sept. 10. Among the many services and features that Apple revealed today, the facts about the new iPhone 11, like the differences between your iPhone 11 and iPhone X models, were possibly the most eagerly anticipated - and the young man did the meeting delivery.

Having a whole new conventional telephone is fun, but could it be worthwhile to ditch your iPhone X (or other older model) for only the shiny new iPhone 11? Well, Perhaps that depends on;

- how practical (or not) your present iPhone model is, and

- if the significant new iPhone 11 features pique your interest or not.

Thankfully, the facts shared in the live stream can make your decision-making a bit easier. Listed below are the five most significant variations between your iPhone X and the iPhone 11 that you will desire to be aware of before deciding if to trade in your old model, in conditions of colours, prices, camera work, and the rest of the major things which were announced. Take note, though, that is just evaluating the iPhone X to the iPhone 11, rather than the other two models which were also announced, the iPhone 11 Pro and iPhone 11 Pro Max, which you can find out about in this book.

1. *iPhone 11 comes in Six Fun, New Colours*

I'm one of these people who cares way too much about the colour of their iPhone's outside - why I had been such a sucker for both (now nearly-vintage) iPhone 5C and my iPhone XR model. With regards to the iPhone 11, we will have a much bigger collection of fun colours to choose from than we did with the iPhone X.

iPhone X came in merely two simple colour options - metallic and space grey. However, the new iPhone 11 comes in six fun colours: *Dark, white, crimson, green, yellowish, and red.* If you are someone who prefers to show off your particular flavour and personality through your phone colour choice, the iPhone 11 will give you a lot more opportunity to do this than the iPhone X.

2. *The iPhone 11 Camera has Some Major Upgrades*

Probably one of the most anticipated feature improvements as it pertains to any new iPhone unveiling involves anything regarding the camera - and iPhone 11's reported improvements do not disappoint. First of all, unlike the iPhone X (or any other previous model, for example), rather than 1X and 2X and the primary zoom options, nowadays, there are three, with ultra-wide represented as a "0.5x" or fifty percent focus. It's choice I find just a little complicated since Samsung describes its three capturing settings with a stand of trees and shrubs: one tree represents 2X, two represents no move and a relatively distant band of three trees and shrubs represents ultra-wide (I honestly can't decide which is more evident).

Even if you're not in the iPhone 11 Pro's new ultra-wide camera mode, the new camera application will always demonstrate the amount of visual information you're abandoning: the dark borders of the camera application turn translucent, and that means you can see the actual ultra-wide zoom lens, which would be added if you were utilizing it.

Apple, also, has introduced a Camera App drawer that you gain access to by swiping up close to the bottom level of the display. Under it, is aspect percentage *(4:3 or 16:9), Live photos, display, filters, HDR*, as well as your timer (I had been a little annoyed that Apple hid it this way). I love the new QuickTake video feature, which enables you to switch from picture set to video by just keeping down the shutter button. After that, you can slip it to them to lock it on while keeping the usage of a photo-in-video button on the right.

3. _There are a few Fun Video Updates, Too_

The camera's perks don't connect with photos alone, of course. There are a few r fun new video functions that come in handy - specifically for those folks who go on Instagram and Snapchat 24/7. First of all, based on the live stream, iPhone 11 gets the highest-quality video of any smartphone out there, so you are getting the best of the greatest.

One fun new feature called _**"QuickTake"**_ gives you to efficiently record brief videos without turning toggles in your camera app. Keep down the picture shutter button (just like you'll when documenting a video within an Instagram tale), and you may take a brief video in the centre of a photo take, and never have to interrupt your circulation and switch to the individual video screen.

Another fun new feature is the capability to record slow-motion footage on leading facing cameras, leading to what Apple knew as a _**"Slofie"**_ (or a slow-motion video selfie). Prepare to up your selfie game in sexy, dramatic,

'80s-music-video-style techniques the iPhone X can't deliver.

4. *iPhone 11 has a Longer Electric Battery Life & Better Speed*

If you are someone who's continually chasing down chargers, excellent news - iPhone 11 is swooping directly in to help us make the majority of our phone's electric battery life by ensuring it's an extended one. Based on the Apple event, the iPhone 11's "all day long battery life" is longer than previous models - and you will be one hour longer than even the iPhone XR's battery life, which at the time had the most extended battery life of any smartphone.

Additionally, it's reported that the iPhone 11 will surpass the iPhone X as long as the effectiveness of both its central processing unit and graphics processing unit, as it possesses the quickest CPU and GPU of any smartphone on the marketplace; this bodes perfectly for the overall speed of the new iPhone and is especially helpful for operating mobile video games (perhaps via the freshly-announced Apple Arcade) if that's your glass o' tea.

5. *iPhone 11 is Cheaper Than Earlier Models*

The purchase price point of a fresh iPhone is nearly always a significant deciding factor as it pertains to if you should trade up, and regarding iPhone 11, this may be working for you. A new iPhone 11 clocks in at $699, which, for a brand-new model's release, seems pretty affordable. It's exceptionally sensible in comparison to the iPhone X's start price, which clocked in at $999, which makes it the priciest new iPhone model today. With this considered, taking the plunge into iPhone 11 and immediately doesn't appear so impossible.

If, after all, iPhone 11 provides sounds peachy by an up-front $699, continues to be unthinkable, the trade-in price for the iPhone 11 drops right down to only $399, or $17 monthly. There you own it, folks - only several most significant differences between your iPhone X and the iPhone 11. Only a reminder that post is evaluating the iPhone 11 with the iPhone X - the other iPhone 11 series models include additional features beyond those explained above and aren't one of them post, nevertheless, you can check them out here.

iPhone 11 vs iPhone XR assessment: What's the difference?

Apple announced the new iPhones at a meeting in Sept 2019, and like this past year, there are three new iPhones to choose from: the iPhone 11, iPhone 11 Pro, and iPhone 11 Pro Max. We have, in comparison, the three new models in another feature, but here we are considering the way the iPhone 11 comes even close to last year's iPhone XR.

Should you update from the iPhone XR, or if you have a mature iPhone, in the event you choose the iPhone XR or the iPhone 11 given, they may be for sale alongside one another?

- *Design*

iPhone 11: 150.9 x 75.7 x 8.3mm, 194g

iPhone XR: 150.9 x 75.7 x 8.3mm, 194g

The iPhone 11 and the iPhone XR both provide a similar design for the reason that they both come in several colours, offer an aluminum frame and a cup rear. There is a notch near the top of both their shows and they're identical in conditions of footprint and weight.

The iPhone XR is IP67 water-resistant, however, enabling it to be submerged up to one meter for thirty minutes, as the iPhone 11 is IP68 rated, offering submergence up to two-metres for thirty minutes. The iPhone 11 also offers a dual rear camera, with a camera casing that has frosted glass to differentiate it from all of those other glossy bodies and the Apple logo design techniques to the centre of the back, with the iPhone working removed entirely. The iPhone XR, in the meantime, has an individual back camera - making for the primary difference in design between both of these handsets - and it gets the Apple logo design higher up the back, as the iPhone branding rests towards underneath.

The colour options also differ between your iPhone 11 and iPhone XR, with the iPhone 11's colours more pastel in their approach and more beautiful because of this. The green and crimson options of the iPhone 11 are lovely, but we are big followers of the coral and blue options in the iPhone XR too.

- *Display*

iPhone 11: 6.1-inch, LCD, 1792 x 828 pixel resolution, no HDR, 625nits

iPhone XR: 6.1-inch, LCD, 1792 x 828 pixel resolution, no HDR, 625nits

Both iPhone 11 and the iPhone XR have a 6.1-in. Water Retina LCD screen, which has a 1792 x 828-pixel quality, producing a pixel denseness of 326ppi.

Nothing at all has changed in conditions of the display as it pertains to the cheaper iPhone models - the iPhone 11 and iPhone XR are identical. True Firmness technology continues to be on board, plus a wide colour gamut, and there continues to be Haptic Touch over 3D Touch. Neither device supplies the punch you will discover on the iPhone 11 Pro models or other OLED smartphones, and there is no HDR either, but you'd only spot the difference if you positioned them side-by-side basic other devices.

Normally, the iPhone 11 and iPhone XR deliver great shows with ample lighting and arguably more realistic colours in comparison to OLED panels.

- *Cameras*

iPhone 11: Tripple back camera (12MP wide position and ultra-wide position), 12MP TrueDepth front side camera

iPhone XR: Solitary back camera (12MP), 7MP TrueDepth entrance camera

One of the primary differences between your iPhone 11 and the iPhone XR is their camera features, with the iPhone 11 the superior device.

The iPhone 11 has a dual-camera on the back, made up of a 12-megapixel ultra-wide-angle sensor with an aperture of f/2.4 and a wide-angle sensor with an aperture of f/1.8. There are optical image stabilization, a brighter True Shade flashes, and Family portrait Light with six results, as well as next-generation Smart HDR for photos. Additionally, there is Nighttime Mode and Auto Adjustments on the iPhone 11, but it is the Evening Mode that is the real stick out feature. The ultra-wide-angle sensor gives you to obtain additional in the shot than you'll get on the iPhone XR, but Night time Mode offers a substantial improvement in low light conditions in comparison to last year's model.

The iPhone XR meanwhile has an individually 12-megapixel rear camera with an f/1.8 aperture, optical image stabilization, and digital zoom up to 5x. Besides, it only offers three results for Portrait Light and first-gen Smart HDR for photos.

The iPhone XR also offers a 7-megapixel TrueDepth camera system with an aperture of f/2.2 on leading, enabling Face Identification, among a lot of other features. It includes 1080p video documenting at 30fps or 60fps.

The iPhone 11, in the meantime, has a 12-megapixel TrueDepth camera on leading, with an aperture of f/2.2, next-gen Smart HDR for photos, and 4K video saving at 24fps, 30fps and 60fps. Gleam slow-motion video option on the iPhone 11's front side camera, enabling what

Apple phone calls **Slofies**. The truth is, this is a reasonably gimmicky feature - like Animoji and Memoji - nevertheless, you can have a blast with it.

- *Hardware*

iPhone 11: A13 chip, 64/256/512GB storage space, Dual SIM

iPhone XR: A12 chip, 64/256/512GB storage space, Dual SIM

Another primary difference between your iPhone 11 and the iPhone XR are hardware. As you'll expect, the iPhone 11 has a bump in hardware, moving from the A12 chip within the iPhone XR to the A13 chip. Both devices are easy in operation; however, the iPhone 11 offers a much better electric battery life than the iPhone XR, even although iPhone XR is, in fact, excellent still.

Both models come in 64GB, 256GB, and 512GB storage space options, though, and microSD for storage space expansion isn't on any model. Both devices support dual SIM with a nano-SIM and eSIM, and both devices are charged via Lightning. Besides, they both offer Apple Pay, plus they both offer 4G, however, not 5G features.

- *Software*

iPhone 11: iOS 13

iPhone XR: iOS 13 compatible

The iPhone 11 brings the release of iOS 13 with it; this means several new features including Dark Setting, a fresh Find My application that combines Find My Friends, and discover My iPhone collectively, a swiping keypad, an overhaul of Reminders and many other updates.

You can read about iOS 13 and what features it includes in greater detail inside our preview. The iPhone XR will also operate on iOS 13 when the program lands on 19 Sept so that it will offer you the same overall consumer experience as the iPhone 11.

The iPhone 11 has several features occasionally that are hardware-based - mainly in the camera department - and for that reason unavailable on the iPhone XR, but overall, the program experience between the unit is identical.

- *Price*

iPhone 11: From $699/£729

iPhone XR: From $599/£629

The iPhone 11 begins at \$699/£729, which is a little cheaper than the telephone XR started at when it launched this past year and every value in comparison with the iPhone 11 Pro models. The iPhone XR will be sold alongside the iPhone 11, starting at \$599/£629, which makes it a cheaper alternative.

Conclusion

The iPhone 11 has several upgrades on the iPhone XR, with the processor and camera features being the primary differences. The look remains mainly the same between your two devices, though, and the screen and software experience is just about identical too.

Improving from the iPhone XR to the iPhone 11, therefore, only offers a lift in camera - that will be enough for a few - and an increase in rate, but in addition to that, you'll get a fairly similar experience this time. Upgrading from a mature iPhone to either the iPhone XR or iPhone 11 will offer you a lot of differences, though you will have to decide if you would like to spend the excess £100 for the camera and processor boosts in the iPhone 11.

The iPhone 11 is an excellent device; however, the iPhone XR is too, so it's possible you'll be happy with either. When you can spend the money for extra £100, the iPhone 11's Evening Mode and supplementary ultra-wide-angle zoom lens are worthwhile, as well as the prolonged battery pack life, but you won't be disappointed with the iPhone XR as it's still a great performer and great value now.

Chapter 11

Useful iPhone 11 Tips & Tricks

Control Your Apple TV With iPhone 11

The Control Focus on the iPhone 11 has an impressive trick: it enables you to regulate your Apple TV if you have one. As long as your iPhone 11 and Apple Television are on a single cellular network, it'll work. Get into Control Centre and then look for the Apple Television button that shows up. Touch it and start managing your Apple Television.

How to Enable USB Restricted Setting on iPhone 11

Apple just built a robust new security feature into the iPhone 11 with the latest version of iOS; this launch is what's known as **USB Restricted Setting** to the iPhone 11. Lately, companies have been making devices that may be connected to an iPhone's USB slot and crack an iPhone's passcode.

To protect from this, Apple has introduced a USB Restricted Setting. USB Restricted Setting disabled data writing between an iPhone and a USB device if the iPhone is not unlocked to get more than one hour; this effectively makes the iPhone breaking boxes ineffective as they may take hours or times to unlock a locked iPhone.

By default, *USB Restricted Mode* is enabled in iOS. But for those who want to disable it, or make sure it hasn't been disabled, go to the *Configurations app* and touch *Face ID & Passcode*. Enter your passcode and then swipe down until you visit a section entitled *"Allow Access When Locked."*

The final toggle in this section is a field that says *"USB Accessories."* The toggle next to them should be turned OFF (white); this implies *USB Restricted Setting* is allowed, and devices can't download or upload data from/to your iPhone if the iPhone is not unlocked to get more than one hour.

Use Two Pane Scenery View

This tip only pertains to the iPhone 11 Pro Max but is cool nonetheless. If you keep your XS device horizontally when using specific applications, you'll see lots of the built-in apps changes to a two-pane setting, including Email and Records. This setting is the main one you observe on an iPad where, for example, you can see a list of all of your records in the Records app while positively reading or editing a single note.

How to stop iPhone 11 Alarms with Your Face

An extremely cool feature of the iPhone 11 is Face ID. It gives you to unlock your phone just by taking a look at it. Face ID also has various other cool features-like that one. Whenever your iPhone 11 or XS security alarm goes off, you could silent it by just picking right up your iPhone and taking a look at it; this tells your iPhone you understand about the arm, and it'll quiet it.

Quickly Disable Face ID

Depending on your geographical area, the police might be able to legally demand you uncover your smartphone at that moment via its facial recognition features. For reasons unknown, facial biometrics aren't protected in the manner fingerprints, and passcodes are; in a few localities. That's why Apple has generated an attribute that lets you quickly disable Face ID in a pinch without going into your settings. Just press the side button five times, and Face ID will be disabled, and you'll need to enter your passcode instead to gain access to your phone.

How to slow the two times click necessary for Apple Pay

Given that the iPhone 11 jettisoned the Touch ID sensor, you confirm your _Apple Pay_ obligations by using Face ID and twice pressing the medial side button. By default, you would need to dual press the medial side button pretty quickly-but it is possible to make things slow down.

To take action, go to *Settings* > *General* > *Availability*. Now scroll right down to Side Button. Privately Button screen, you can select between *default, gradual, or slowest.* Pick the speed that is most effective for you.

INDEX

www.ingramcontent.com/pod-product-compliance
Ingram Content Group UK Ltd.
Pitfield, Milton Keynes, MK11 3LW, UK
UKHW020112080525
5796UKWH00041B/885